I FEEL SHY

BY STEPHANIE FINNE

BLUE OWL
BOOKS

TIPS FOR CAREGIVERS

Social and emotional learning (SEL) helps children manage emotions, create and achieve goals, maintain relationships, learn how to feel empathy, and make good decisions. The SEL approach will help children establish positive habits in communication, cooperation, and decision-making. By incorporating SEL in early reading, children will be better equipped to build confidence and foster positive peer networks.

BEFORE READING

Talk to the reader about how shyness feels.

Discuss: What makes you feel shy? How does shyness feel in your body?

AFTER READING

Talk to the reader about things he or she can do to overcome shyness.

Discuss: What can you do to prepare for situations that make you shy? How can you build confidence for new situations?

SEL GOAL

Some students may struggle with confidence. They may not be able to see their strengths. Help readers develop a vocabulary to voice their feelings. Help them learn to pause and think about what they are good at and how that makes them feel. Help them build confidence by acknowledging their achievements and hard work.

TABLE OF CONTENTS

CHAPTER 1

FEELING SHY

Do you feel nervous around new people? Do you avoid new **situations**? Maybe you do everything possible to not be noticed. These are examples of shyness.

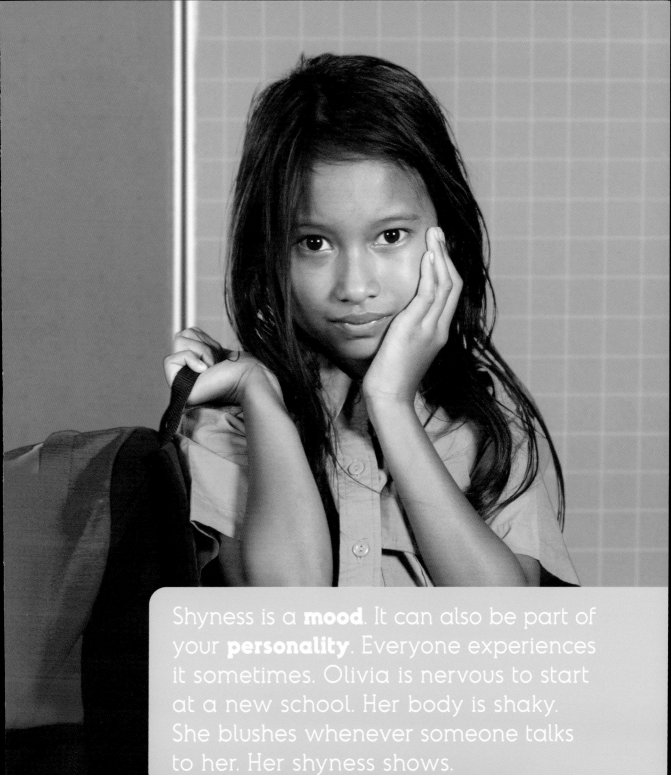

Shyness is a **mood**. It can also be part of your **personality**. Everyone experiences it sometimes. Olivia is nervous to start at a new school. Her body is shaky. She blushes whenever someone talks to her. Her shyness shows.

Being shy can make you feel nervous, **self-conscious**, or **embarrassed**. This can make you feel breathless. Shyness can affect how you act around others. Maybe you don't feel **confident**. You may talk softly.

SHY PERSONALITIES

Some people are shier than others. Some of us have **introverted** personalities. Some of us are **extroverted**.

Body language can show shyness, too. At family gatherings, Emmett doesn't want to be noticed. He looks down. He tries not to make **eye contact** with anyone. He wraps his arms around himself to appear as small as possible.

CHAPTER 2

WHAT CAUSES SHYNESS?

It helps to be **mindful** of what makes you feel shy. Meeting new people makes Ada shy. A new dancer joins her ballet class. She wants to say hi, but she is nervous.

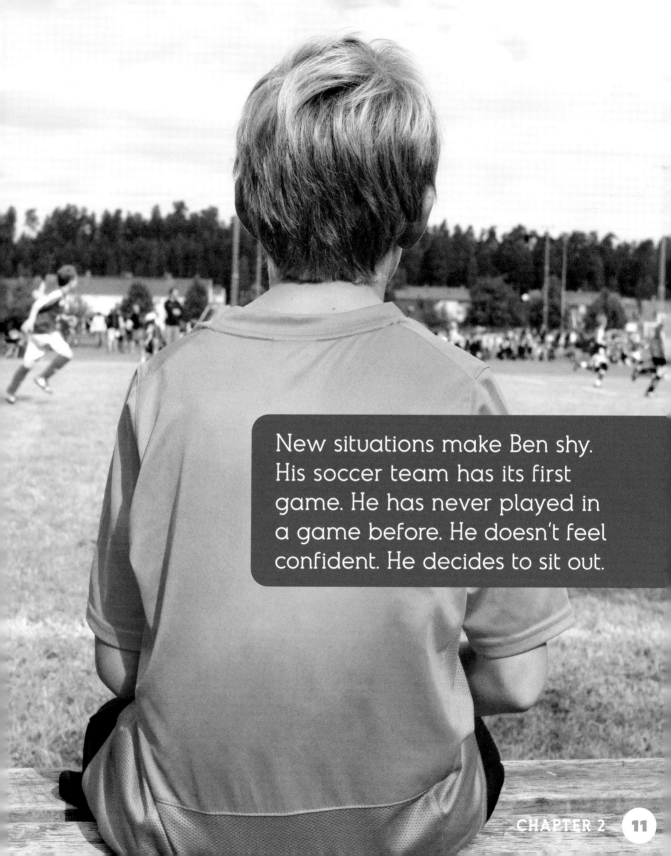

New situations make Ben shy. His soccer team has its first game. He has never played in a game before. He doesn't feel confident. He decides to sit out.

You can feel shy because you don't know how to act. You may be unsure of how others will respond. When you are shy, you may not like attention on you.

Kieran is performing a solo at the spring concert. He is nervous about performing in front of a big group. He takes deep breaths to calm himself.

SNEAKY SHYNESS

No one decides to be shy. It just happens. It can sneak up on you. You might feel fine one minute but get nervous when someone approaches.

Being **bullied** can make you feel even more shy. Why? It can make you feel self-conscious about your differences.

Vivi usually feels shy, so she doesn't talk much. One day on the bus, she is teased for being so quiet. Vivi doesn't know what to say in response. She talks even less.

CHAPTER 3

HOW TO SHAKE SHYNESS

It is OK to be shy. But shyness can stop you from connecting with others. It can also stop you from trying new things. **Reflect** on what makes you feel shy. Writing about it might help you face your shyness.

Build confidence by practicing with people you trust. Practice making eye contact and using confident body language, such as standing tall with your hands on your hips.

Try talking to someone new. How do you start? Introduce yourself or ask a question. You could tell your classmate you like her art project or ask what her favorite color is.

POSITIVE SELF-TALK

Practice **positive self-talk**. How? When you're not feeling confident, think about what you would tell your best friend when he or she is down. Then, tell yourself that!

It might feel hard at first, but keep trying! Find a group activity you like. Do something you enjoy. Use this time to get to know new people slowly. The most important thing is to be yourself. Don't let your shyness hold you back. How will you work to shake your shyness?

GOALS AND TOOLS

GROW WITH GOALS

Anyone can feel shy at times. Try these goals to help you build confidence.

Goal: Be mindful of situations that make you feel shy. Make a list of times you felt shy and how it felt at the time.

Goal: Talk to a trusted adult about what makes you feel shy. Ask the adult to help you practice ways to feel more confident in those situations.

Goal: Practice, practice, practice! Take small steps every day to build confidence. Practice making eye contact, introducing yourself, and asking questions.

TRY THIS!

Sometimes it helps to practice situations before they happen. You can role-play to prepare what you will say or do the next time you feel shy. Ask an adult you trust to walk through situations that make you nervous, such as talking to someone new. Practice all the things that could happen so you are prepared for anything.

GLOSSARY

body language
The gestures, movements, and mannerisms by which people communicate with others.

bullied
Frightened or picked on.

confident
Self-assured and having a strong belief in your own abilities.

embarrassed
Ashamed and uncomfortable.

extroverted
Having an outgoing nature.

eye contact
The act of looking someone else straight in the eyes.

introverted
Having a reserved or shy nature.

mindful
A mentality achieved by focusing on the present moment and calmly recognizing and accepting your feelings, thoughts, and sensations.

mood
An emotion that lasts longer than a few minutes.

personality
All of the qualities or traits that make a person different from others.

positive self-talk
Words or thoughts to yourself that make you feel good about yourself and your abilities.

reflect
To think carefully or seriously about something.

self-conscious
Constantly worried about how you look to other people and what they are thinking.

situations
Circumstances that exist at particular times and places.

TO LEARN MORE

FACT SURFER

Finding more information is as easy as 1, 2, 3.

1. Go to www.factsurfer.com

2. Enter "Ifeelshy" into the search box.

3. Choose your book to see a list of websites.

INDEX

Blue Owl Books are published by Jump!, 5357 Penn Avenue South, Minneapolis, MN 55419, www.jumplibrary.com

Copyright © 2022 Jump! International copyright reserved in all countries. No part of this book may be reproduced in any form without written permission from the publisher.

Library of Congress Cataloging-in-Publication Data

Names: Finne, Stephanie, author.
Title: I feel shy / by Stephanie Finne.
Description: Minneapolis, MN: Jump!, Inc., [2022]
Series: States of mind | Includes index. | Audience: Ages 7–10
Identifiers: LCCN 2020054271 (print)
LCCN 2020054272 (ebook)
ISBN 9781636901114 (hardcover)
ISBN 9781636901121 (paperback)
ISBN 9781636901138 (ebook)
Subjects: LCSH: Bashfulness in children–Juvenile literature. | Bashfulness–Juvenile literature.
Classification: LCC BF723.B3 F56 2022 (print) | LCC BF723.B3 (ebook) | DDC 155.4/18232–dc23
LC record available at https://lccn.loc.gov/2020054271
LC ebook record available at https://lccn.loc.gov/2020054272

Editor: Eliza Leahy
Designer: Michelle Sonnek

Photo Credits: Samuel Borges Photography/Shutterstock, cover, 1; Anatoliy Karlyuk/Shutterstock, 3; Krakenimages.com/Shutterstock, 4; TheVisualsYouNeed/Shutterstock, 5; Kues/Shutterstock, 6–7; Gelpi/Shutterstock, 8–9 (foreground); Dusan Petkovic/Shutterstock, 8–9 (background); jocic/Shutterstock, 10 (left); Happy Together/Shutterstock, 10 (right); Michael715/Shutterstock, 11; Maica/iStock, 12–13; LightField Studios/Shutterstock, 14–15, 18–19; MidoSemsem/Shutterstock, 16; wavebreakmedia/Shutterstock, 17; Sergey Novikov/Shutterstock, 20–21.

Printed in the United States of America at Corporate Graphics in North Mankato, Minnesota.